MW00709766

Freebies

for Teachers ®

Also available from Lowell House:

The Official Freebies® for Families

The Official Freebies® for Kids

The Official

Freebies for Teachers

By the Editors of *Freebies* Magazine

Illustrations by Wesla Weller

Lowell House
Los Angeles

Contemporary Books
Chicago

Copyright © 1993 by Freebies Publishing Company
All rights reserved. No part of this work may be reproduced or transmitted in any form
or by any means, electronic or mechanical, including photocopying and recording, or by
any information storage or retrieval system, except as may be expressly permitted by the
1976 Copyright Act or in writing by the publisher.

Requests for such permissions should be addressed to:
Lowell House
2029 Century Park East, Suite 3290
Los Angeles, CA 90067

ISBN: 1-56565-060-3
Library of Congress Catalog Card Number: 92-44298

Manufactured in the United States of America

10 9 8 7 6 5 4 3 2 1

Why FREEBIES ??

"Why are they giving it away?" No matter what you do, giving potential customers a sample is a great way to attract attention to a product. If the product is good, a satisfied customer may tell as many as 10 people about it.

About this Book

FREEBIES for Teachers presents more than 150 freebie offers that you can get through the mail. The *FREEBIES* editors reviewed hundreds of offers before selecting the offers for this book. Each offer is written to describe the freebie as accurately as possible. Unlike other "get things free" books, we have confirmed with each supplier that they want to be listed in this book and each supplier of each offer has agreed to have an adequate stock to honor all properly made requests. The suppliers have also agreed to fill all requests through 1993. Due to fluctuating economic conditions, requests made after 1993 may not be honored.

How to Use this Book

1. *Follow the directions:* Each offer specifies how to order the freebie. Some offers specifically request a postcard (the U.S. Post Office will not process 3 x 5 index cards in lieu of a postcard). Other offers may ask for an SASE (a long self-addressed, stamped envelope with the requested postage). If a fee is requested, include the proper amount (a check or money order is usually preferred). Use a single piece of tape to affix any coins. A few suppliers may wait for out-of-town checks to clear before filling orders.

2. *Print all information:* Not everyone's handwriting is easy to read. It is safer to neatly print your name, address, and the complete spelling of your city on your request. Be sure to include your return address on the outside of your mailing envelope or postcard. Use a ballpoint pen, typewriter, or computer to make your requests. Pencil can often smear, felt tip or ink pens smudge easily.

3. Allow time for your request to be processed and sent: Some suppliers send their offers via first-class mail. Others use bulk-mail and this can take up to six or eight weeks. Our suppliers get thousands of requests each year and depending on the time of the year may process slower or faster than at other times.

4. What to do if you are unhappy: If you are dissatisfied or have complaints about an offer, let us know. If you have not received your offer within eight to ten weeks of your request, let us know. Although we do not stock the items or offer refunds from our offices, we follow up on your complaints with any supplier. Occasionally there are problems with a particular supplier or offer. Your letters alert us to these problems. Suppliers that generate too many complaints will not be included in future editions. Send your complaints, comments, or suggestions, to:

> FREEBIES Book Editors
> 1135 Eugenia Place
> Carpinteria, CA 93014

5. And There Are More FREEBIES: If you like the freebie offers you see in this book and want to see more great freebies, then you should subscribe to *FREEBIES Magazine*. Five times a year, *FREEBIES* sends you a great magazine filled with 100 freebies in each issue. Purchasers of *Freebies for Teachers* can get a special price on a one-year/five-issue subscription of only $5.00 (the regular subscription rate is $8.95—you'll save almost $4.00). See the special offer on page 79.

Acknowledgments

It is difficult to put together a book of this type without the help of talented and dedicated people working together. The staff at *FREEBIES* has a special thank you for the commitment of RGA/Lowell House Publishing to this project. Their support made it happen.

Special thanks are reserved for Abigail Koehring for research and to Donald Weiner and Margaret Koike for the writing and editing. Special thanks are also accorded to Linda Cook for all of her hard work and attention to detail.

Special mention must also be given to Bud Sperry, Peter Hoffman, Mary Aarons, Brenda Leach, and the rest of the professionals at RGA/Lowell House for the final editing, design, and labor to complete the project.

Rubber Stamps
Instant Art

☆ Even if art isn't your forte, you can use these **quality rubber stamps** to make picture-perfect images on your students' homework assignments or work.

You will receive two unmounted rubber stamps; if you wish, use rubber cement to mount them on bottle caps or small pieces of wood. Now grab an ink pad and stamp away!

Send: A long SASE with two first-class stamps affixed

Ask For: Two rubber stamps (Please specify your favorite animal and hobby)

Mail To: Ramastamps—K
7924 Soper Hill Road
Everett, WA 98205

Educational Brochure
Reach for the Stars

☆ Astronomy, the world's oldest science, may offer the perfect profession for students interested in math and physics. You and they will learn more about a career in this field when you send for the **24-page brochure** titled *Understanding the Universe: A Career in Astronomy.*

The brochure explains what astronomers do and how young people can prepare themselves for careers as an astronomer. The publication also lists schools that offer advanced programs in astronomy.

Send: 50¢ postage & handling

Ask For: *Understanding the Universe: A Career in Astronomy*

Mail To: AAS Education Office
University of Texas
Dept. of Astronomy, RLM 15.308
Austin, TX 78712-1083

Coloring Books
Color Us Friends

☆ The **You and Your Kitten** or **You and Your Puppy coloring book** will help show a young pet owner how to care for his or her cuddly new friend—and how to respect canines and felines.

Each fun 8 1/2" x 11" coloring book includes games, illustrations, and instructions on handling a new pet.

Send: Your name & address

Ask For: Either *You and Your Kitten* or *You and Your Puppy* coloring book

Mail To: The ALPO Pet Center
P.O. Box 25200
Lehigh Valley, PA 18002-5200

Memo Clips
Creature Clips

☆ You've heard the term "gorilla grip" before and no doubt you've heard of alligator clips, too. But you've probably never seen **memo clips** that fit these terms as literally as these.

These fun memo clips come in an assortment of animal designs (supplier's choice) as varied as nature itself. There are brightly colored gorillas, hippos, walruses, and others, each sporting a silly grin. These plastic clips have a sturdy metal spring and a hole that makes them perfect for handing papers from blackboard hooks.

Send: $1.65 postage & handling for three

Ask For: Animal memo clips

Mail To: Marlene Monroe
Dept. Memo clips
6210 Ridge Manor Drive
Memphis, TN 38115-3411

Kids' Audio Magazine

Awesome Audio

☆ Inspire your students with stories, jokes, mysteries, and current events compiled by kids just like them. Request an issue of *BOOMERANG!*, **a magazine that comes on a cassette tape.**

This innovative, 70-minute audiocassette turns short stories, world affairs, history, and other interesting topics into a media happening.

Send: $2.00 postage & handling

Ask For: *BOOMERANG!* free issue

Mail To: *BOOMERANG!* magazine
123 Townsend Street, Suite 636-F
San Francisco, CA 94107

Word Puzzle

Brain Baffler

☆ Send for a free, autographed *Brain Baffler* puzzle and see how fast you and your English class can find the hidden words and arrange the leftover letters in this tough brainteaser.

Created by 20-year-old Jodi Jill, one of the youngest syndicated newspaper columnists in America, this **mind-boggling puzzle** has stumped some of the cleverest minds.

Send: A long SASE

Ask For: *Brain Baffler* puzzle

Mail To: Free Puzzle
Attn. Jodi Jill
2888 Bluff Street, Suite 143
Boulder, CO 80301

Publication

Checkmate!

☆ Children and adults all over the world enjoy chess, the king of board games. Chess develops one's ability to think both analytically and strategically, and it complements academic pursuits.

You and your class can learn the official rules of this challenging game by consulting the **pamphlet Let's Play Chess.** A second publication *Let's Get Moving* invites kids to join the U.S. Chess Federation.

Send: A long SASE

Ask For: *Let's Play Chess* and *Let's Get Moving*

Mail To: Ms. Barbara A. DeMaro
U.S. Chess Federation
186 Rte. 9W
New Windsor, NY 12553

Recipes & Coupon

Chocolate Fever

☆ Calling all chocoholics! This pamphlet, filled with **ten chocolate chunk cookie recipes and a store coupon,** will have you and your students concocting a little kitchen chemistry. You'll find that the delectable, naturally flavored, semisweet chocolate chunks are perfect for all of the cookie recipes in this offer.

Send: A long SASE

Ask For: Chocolate chunk cookie recipes & store coupon

Mail To: SACO Foods
Freebies cookie offer
P.O. Box 616
Middleton, WI 53562

Or call toll-free: 1-800-373-SACO

Scented Stickers

Scent-sational Stickers

☆ These cute **teddy bear scratch 'n sniff stickers** will spice up students' notebooks, folders, and letters. Smelling like cinnamon candy sticks, the round decals come in six different designs on 4-1/2" x 6" sheets.

Choose one sheet of 88 stickers or three sheets of 264 stickers—plenty for you to use as incentives for beary wonderful work.

Send: $1.00 for 88; or $2.00 for 264

Ask For: Teddy bear scratch 'n sniff stickers: 88 or 264

Mail To: The Very Best
Dept. TB
P.O. Box 2838
Long Beach, CA 90801-2838

Herb Seeds

Spice of Life

☆ Start a classroom herb garden with this **package of five different herb seeds:** sage, French sorrel, parsley, bouquet dill, and Italian basil. Get out your green thumbs and have fun teaching and learning about both botany and gastronomy!

Send: $1.00 postage & handling

Ask For: Herb seeds package

Mail To: Clyde Robin Herbs
P.O. Box 57043
Hayward, CA 94545

Sample Copy of Children's Publications

Magazine Mania

☆ Respond to this great offer and you will receive a **sample copy** of one of the following six magazines: *Turtle Magazine* (for 3- to 4-year-olds), *Humpty Dumpty* (for 4- to 5-year-olds), *Children's Playmate* (for 6- to 8-year-olds), *Jack & Jill* (for 7- to 10-year-olds), *Child Life* (for 9- to 11-year-olds), and *Children's Digest* (for 10- to 12-year-olds).

All of the magazines feature colorful illustrations and a question and answer column.

Send: $1.25 postage & handling for each

Ask For: The magazine's title

Mail To: Children's Better Health Institute
Attn: Jeanne Aydt, Sample "F"
1100 Waterway Blvd.
Indianapolis, IN 46206

Instruction Sheets

Hot Invention

☆ Here's a hot idea for a cool science fair project or a sizzling summer activity. It's a **solar hot dog cooker** that you can make from materials you have around your home or classroom.

Send for this four-page set of simple instructions for making a sun-powered hot dog cooker from cardboard and tin foil. Your students will enjoy constructing the reflector-cooker and eating the sun-cooked dogs.

Send: A long SASE and 25¢

Ask For: Instruction manual for making a solar hot dog cooker

Mail To: Energy & Marine Center
P.O. Box 190
Port Richey, FL 34673

School Kit

Back to School

☆ Here's a **kit to welcome new students** that you can afford. You'll receive two rainbow heart or fruit erasers (supplier's choice), and a 6-inch ruler. The ruler has a small magnifying lens built into it and displays metric, as well as linear scales.

Send: $2.00 for one set; or $15.00 for ten sets

Ask For: Back to school kit

Mail To: Neetstuf
Dept. S-7
P.O. Box 459
Stone Harbor, NJ 08247

Comic Book

In a Nutshell

☆ With *The Gold Peanut* **comic book,** young geographers and botanists can follow the adventures of Eric and Anna in South America's Chicma River Valley as the pair learn all about peanuts.

Published by the National Peanut Council, the 16-page comic book will surprise kids with fascinating facts about the nut that's not really a nut.

Send: Two first-class postage stamps

Ask For: *The Gold Peanut* comic book

Mail To: Peanuts
P.O. Box 1709
Rocky Mount, NC 27802-1709

Harmonica Booklet
New Notes

☆ The *How to Play the Marine Band-Type Hohner Harmonica* **booklet** is a simple, 24-page guide for those who want to learn to play the harmonica, an instrument perfect for impromptu classroom concerts. Follow the numbers and arrows in the booklet and play popular, well-loved tunes.

Send: A long SASE

Ask For: *How to Play the Marine Band-Type Hohner Harmonica*

Mail To: Dept. FD
Hohner, Inc.
P.O. Box 9375
Richmond, VA 23227

Newspaper
Kindness Counts

☆ Kids *can* make a difference! Show your students how. Pass around an issue of *KIND News*, **a monthly newspaper** from the Kids in Nature's Defense Club.

Published by the National Association for Humane and Environmental Education, the illustrated, four-page periodical promotes kindness to animals, people, and the environment. Choose the junior or senior version.

Send: A long SASE plus 50¢ postage & handling

Ask For: *KIND News Jr.* (grades 2–4) or *KIND News Sr.* (grades 5–6)

Mail To: KIND News
Dept. FF
67 Salem Rd.
East Haddam, CT 06423-1736

Key Chain or Pen

Batter Up

☆ We're sure that when you present this **Louisville Slugger**® **bat pen** or **bat key chain** as an incentive, your offer will prompt kids to score high on tests or homework assignments.

Because each plastic, 5-inch replica of a real Slugger bat is certain to be a home-run hit, you'll score high with your students, too.

Send: $1.00 postage & handling for each

Ask For: Louisville Slugger® bat pen or bat key chain

Mail To: H & B Promotions
Dept. Freebies
P.O. Box 10
Jeffersonville, IN 47130

"No Smoking" Sign

Lungs at Work

☆ Protect your students' right to breathe clean air! Post this **clever sign that reads, "Lungs at Work, No Smoking."**

Produced by the American Lung Association, the friendly red and white reminder looks like a small, octagonal stop sign.

Send: Your name & address

Ask For: "No Smoking" sign

Mail To: American Lung Association
P.O. Box 596-FB, #0121
New York, NY 10116-0596

Rat Newsletter

Oh, Rats!

☆ Rats have had a bad rap! Help set the record straight and learn about these friendly critters by reading **a sample issue of *The Rat Report*,** an informative publication created by the "big cheese" at a state university rat lab.

This interesting newsletter explains the benefits of having rats as pets and answers questions about choosing, training, and caring for these intelligent, clean rodents that make great classroom pals.

Send: A long SASE

Ask For: Sample issue of *The Rat Report* newsletter

Mail To: PET-ABLES
1010-1/2 Broadway
Chico, CA 95928

Clothing Dye Ideas

Quick Change

☆ Turn your old duds into a sensational new wardrobe by following the instructions in *Grade A Looks With Rit® Dye.* Put together your own dye-namic outfits or use the **eight-page booklet**'s ideas to initiate classroom art projects.

The publication explains how to transform old jeans, T-shirts, and sweats by dipping them in dye baths.

Send: Your name & address

Ask For: *Grade A Looks With Rit® Dye*

Mail To: Grade A Looks With Rit® Dye
Dept. 231
P.O. Box 307
Coventry, CT 06238

Button & Poster
Hand Talk

☆ Learn and teach how to "speak" the alphabet with your hands; read and follow this **8-1/2" x 11" sign language alphabet poster** printed on card stock.

This offer also includes a fashionable, bright yellow, 3-inch button showing the hand positions of each letter of the alphabet.

Once you learn the sign-language alphabet, you'll be able to communicate more effectively with your hearing impaired students and colleagues.

Send: $2.00 postage & handling

Ask For: Sign language alphabet poster & button

Mail To: Keep Quiet
P.O. Box 367
Stanhope, NJ 07874

Stickers
Positive Appeal

☆ Sometimes a small word of encouragement is all that's needed to push an underachieving student to their potential. These **1/4" round positive word stickers** are a great way to express your care and pride for your students.

The colorful little stickers come 96 to a sheet with six different dynamic designs with words: wow, super, tops, neat, first-rate, and hot.

Send: $1.00 postage & handling for 96; $2.00 for 288

Ask For: Positive word stickers

Mail To: The Very Best
Dept. PW
P.O. Box 2838
Long Beach, CA 90801

Ruler

To Create With

☆ This item creates a high-level of child participation and creativity. It's an **8" x 3-1/2" inch ruler.** In the center section are three pop-out, gear-edged circles of plastic, each of which has many small holes through its solid surface. In addition, there are two large circular openings on the ruler, each with a geared border. By putting a pencil or pen point through one of the pop-out circles, and moving it around, all sorts of fancy, lace-like designs can be created. Perfect for the six- to sixteen-year old with an artistic, mechanical drawing, or doodling flair.

Send: $1.50 postage & handling; $11.50 for ten

Ask For: Design ruler

Mail To: Mr. Rainbows
Dept. S-6
P.O. Box 387
Avalon, NJ 08202

Word Puzzle

Crossword Smarts

☆ Send for *Let's Solve the Smokeword Puzzle* and challenge your high schoolers to solve this challenging brainteaser.

Produced by the American Lung Association, this **tough crossword puzzle** imparts wisdom while it uses smart "no-smoking" slogans in its clues.

Send: Your name & address

Ask For: *Let's Solve the Smokeword Puzzle*

Write To: American Lung Association
P.O. Box 596-FB #0071
New York, NY 10116-0596

Book

Racing Dreams

☆ Give your kids a project and a purpose. Help them drive to victory in soapbox derby racers that they built themselves. How to begin? Request this thorough *All-American Soapbox Derby* **book** and learn how boys and girls can compete in exciting derbies on the local and national levels.

The 22-page book includes photos of the race winners and the cars they constructed. So get your racers to start their engines!

Send: Your name & address

Ask For: *All-American Soapbox Derby* book

Mail To: All-American Soapbox Derby
P.O. Box 7233
Akron, OH 44306

Spanish Lesson

Se habla español

☆ ¡Hola! Beginning Spanish speakers can learn some new vocabulary words and follow an authentic Latin American recipe when they read this free issue of the **Spanish lesson newsletter** called *Bueno*.

Appropriate for home or classroom, the eight-page, quarterly publication makes learning Spanish a snap. It teaches words in both English and Spanish and includes phonetic spellings of Spanish words.

Send: A long SASE

Ask For: *Bueno* Spanish lesson newsletter

Mail To: Lesson
Dept. FM
29481 Manzanita Dr.
Campo, CA 91906

Whale Kit

Take a Whale to School

☆ This **Whales of the World kit** offers fun activities and all sorts of fascinating facts about the gentle giants of the sea.

Appropriate for students of all ages, the kit includes activity sheets, a glossary of terms, and a teacher's guide. The package also provides information on how your school or class can adopt its very own whale through the Whale Adoption Project, a nonprofit organization.

Send: $1.00 postage & handling

Ask For: *Whales of the World* teaching kit

Mail To: Whale Adoption Project
P.O. Box 388
North Falmouth, MA 02556-0388

Tips Booklet

No Waffling

☆ If your students "waffle" or dawdle in the morning, you need a copy of this **helpful booklet** from Aunt Jemima Waffles. Titled *Getting Kids Off to a Good Start: Morning Wake-up Tips from Aunt Jemima Waffles*, the six-panel publication supplies great tips for easing the morning rush.

Perfect for sharing with parents, the illustrated booklet discusses routines, time cushions, and ways to wake sleepy heads. It also offers a couple of tasty recipes that include Aunt Jemima frozen waffles.

Send: A long SASE

Ask For: *Aunt Jemima Morning Tips*

Mail To: "Aunt Jemima Morning Tips"
P.O. Box 1064
Maple Plain, MN 55592   **Limit:** One per address

Bookmarks

Hear & There

☆ Teach your students how to communicate with people who have a hearing loss while you communicate your appreciation for their good work. Send for this set of **25 colorful deafness awareness bookmarks** in four different designs, then use them as rewards for jobs well done.

The bookmarks simply and clearly introduce hearing loss, the manual alphabet, and sign language.

Send: $1.00 postage & handling

Ask For: 25 deafness awareness bookmarks

Mail To: National Information Center on Deafness
Freebies Offer/Gallaudet
800 Florida Avenue, NE
Washington, DC 20002

Poster

The New World

☆ Recreate for students the story of the pilgrims who settled the original American colonies. These **historical parchments** are teaching aids that illustrate the historical events of the pilgrims' landing. Choose the official "Mayflower Compact," or a recounting of the "Landing of the Pilgrims." Both are printed on parchment paper that adds a genuine historical quality, making them perfect for use as props in school plays and reenactments.

Send: $1.75 postage & handling for one; $3.00 for both;
or $20.00 for 20 (mix or match)

Ask For: Mayflower Compact or Landing of the pilgrims

Mail To: Neetstuf
Dept. S-12
P.O. Box 459
Stone Harbor, NJ 08247

Bottle & Can Openers

Great Gizmos

☆ If you've ever waged war with a stubborn lid on a bottle or can, you'll recognize the value in these two **combination bottle and can openers.** One end of each 1-3/8" x 3" plastic gizmo keeps fingernails intact by lifting pop tops on aluminum cans; the other end boasts a notched ring for opening twist-off bottle caps, thus preventing hand pain.

Keep one of these devices in your car, purse, or briefcase; hang the other in the teachers' lounge so that everyone will benefit.

Send: $1.00 postage & handling for two

Ask For: Two combination bottle & can openers

Mail To: Specialty Marketing
10812 Petit
Granada Hills, CA 91344

Key Chain Kit

Concho Craft

☆ Here's your art or geography class's key to fashion and fun: **a concho key chain kit** that each child can easily turn into a unique, Southwestern-style accessory.

Perfect for boys or girls, each kit includes a 1-1/2" silver-colored concho (a disk decorated with a simple native American design); a 14" leather thong, six silver-colored beads; a key ring; and complete, illustrated instructions.

Send: $1.75 postage & handling

Ask For: Concho key chain kit

Mail To: Scribbles & Giggles
1402 Woodland Drive
Santa Paula, CA 93060

Recipe Folder

Dino Dining

☆ This **fantasy-filled recipe folder** will have youngsters requesting healthy canned pears for every meal—and asking plenty of questions about the lizards who lived eons ago. Titled *Dining with Dinosaurs*, the fully illustrated, fold-out publication encourages kids to imagine just how a Brontopearus, Pearannosaurus, Pearasaurolophus, and Pearodactyl might use a can of pears.

Because the folder's concept is so intriguing and the recipes so simple, your pupils will want to prepare prehistoric pear fare all by themselves.

Send: A long SASE

Ask For: *Dining with Dinosaurs* recipe folder

Mail To: Dinosaur
CFPS, Inc.
P.O. Box 7111
San Francisco, CA 94120

Poster

All the Presidents

☆ This 13-1/2" x 16" **poster** printed on parchment-like paper looks and feels like an antique. However, the information on it is current. It contains the picture, signature, and date each President was in office. It is big enough to hang in your classroom for all to see.

Send: $1.75 postage & handling

Ask For: Presidential Parchment

Mail To: Neetstuf
Dept. S-9
P.O. Box 459
Stone Harbor, NJ 08247

Product Catalog
Natural Pride

☆ The environmentally responsible company called Earth Pride International is "doing a world of good" by offering folks recycled and earth-preserving products—and by supporting organizations that will improve the environment for kids everywhere.

So send for a full-color *Earth Pride Products* catalog and see the kinds of biodegradable cleaners and personal care products that can help protect our world for the next generation.

Send: $1.00 postage & handling

Ask For: *Earth Pride Products* catalog

Mail To: Sandpoint International
P.O. Box 872, Dept. F
Marion, IA 52302

Flower Seeds
Growing Passion

☆ Here's a passion that you can exhibit even at school, and it may provoke a growing passion in your pupils. It arises from a **package of Passion flower seeds,** which develop into the fast-growing South American vines with their many glossy green leaves, climbing tendrils, and beautiful flowers.

So plant the seeds of passion and watch them grow—up to four inches a day.

Send: $1.00 postage & handling

Ask For: Passion flower seeds

Mail To: Passion Flower
P.O. Box 3498
San Rafael, CA 94902

Toy Brochure

Wooden Wonders

☆ Discover toys that teach, entertain and challenge; take a look at this fun-to-read, **colorful brochure of wooden toys** from the Elwood Turner Company.

The company produces delightful, safe, hardwood playthings that are perfect for homes, day-care centers, or classrooms. The 12-page brochure even offers three innovative games that will fascinate grownups.

Send: $1.00 postage & handling (refunded with purchase)

Ask For: Colorful brochure of wooden toys

Mail To: Elwood Turner Co.
Dept. F-1
P.O. Box HC 132
Morrisville, VT 05661

Foil Glitz Pencils

The Write Way

☆ Motivate kids to do their homework: reward them with writing instruments that make the process fun. Request pairs of **foil glitz pencils** that will keep your students' fingers energized and their eyes riveted on the assignments at hand.

The standard-size, iridescent pencils come in **assorted** colors.

Send: $1.00 postage & handling

Ask For: Two foil glitz pencils

Mail To: Peggy's Stuff
Box 274
Avon, MA 02322-0274

Name Tag Stickers

Happy & You Know It

☆ "If you're happy and you know it, then your face will surely show it," and so will your Happy Face name tags.

Use these **40 merry labels** on the first day of school, at PTA meetings, for birthday parties, at Scout meetings, or whenever you need to identify smiling new faces. Each 2-1/4" x 2-3/4" self-adhesive white tag carries a border of multicolored happy faces.

Send: $2.00 postage & handling

Ask For: 40 happy face name tags

Mail To: S. Brown
P.O. Box 568
Techny, IL 60082

Health Booklet

Sneaky Snacks

☆ Do you sabotage your health by snacking between classes? According to the helpful **booklet** titled *Sneak Health into Your Snacks*, the right snacks can actually benefit your body.

This 30-page publication from the American Institute for Cancer Research educates eaters by offering snacking strategies and listing substitutes for high-fat nibbles.

Once you've digested its healthful information about "grazing" sensibly, you can pass along your knowledge to your students.

Send: A long SASE with 52¢ postage affixed

Ask For: *Sneak Health into Your Snacks*

Mail To: American Institute for Cancer Research—Dept. HS
Washington, DC 20069

Student Guide

Aid to Animals

☆ You'd be amazed at how students working together can help protect the environment and endangered animals. Published by the Humane Society of the United States, the **HSUS Student Action Guide** provides some inspirational examples of student action and explains how children and teenagers can make a significant difference on our earth.

Send: Your name & address

Ask For: *HSUS Student Action Guide*

Mail To: HSUS Youth Education Division
Dept. FF
67 Salem Road
East Haddam, CT 06423-1736

Science Glasses

Rose-Colored Glasses

☆ We call them rainbow glasses. They are **brightly colored, cardboard glasses** with lenses made of holographic diffraction grating. Excellent for use in the science classroom for a lesson on light and light diffraction, and for the emerging artist who can use it to see the light spectrum of various light sources. You will receive three pairs of rainbow glasses and an informative little booklet which describes light information and various uses for the glasses.

Send: $2.00 for two pair; $15.00 for twenty

Ask For: Rainbow glasses

Mail To: Mr. Rainbows
Dept. S-11
P.O. Box 387
Avalon, NJ 08202

Publications
Disabilities Info

☆ You and your colleagues will be interested in these **publications** from the Learning Disabilities Association of America, particularly if you teach students with special educational needs.

When Learning Is a Problem is a brochure that discusses the signs of and potential solutions for learning disabilities, and *LDA Newsbriefs* offers the latest information on resources, research, and events in the field.

Send: Your name & address

Ask For: Learning Disabilities Association brochure & LDA Newsbriefs

Mail To: LDA
4156 Library Road
Pittsburgh, PA 15234

Erasers
No Wrong Notes

☆ Rub out errors while you proclaim your love of music; use one of three assorted **musical instrument erasers** to eliminate wrong notes from your own work—or to reward the best efforts in your students' repertoire.

Cut in the shape of a popular instrument, each white eraser measures about 1-1/2" long and carries a colorful representation of that particular music-maker.

Send: $1.50 postage & handling for three

Ask For: Set of three assorted musical instrument erasers (Supplier's choice)

Mail To: Marlene Monroe
6219 Ridge Manor Drive
Memphis, TN 38115

Sewing Booklet

Penny-wise Patterns

☆ Move from miniature pattern to full-scale masterpiece when you and your students consult the economical, clearly written *Patterns for Pennies*, a **booklet** that shows readers how to sew 20 different classic patterns for children and adults.

The booklet also includes easy instructions for enlarging patterns quickly by using grids.

Send: $2.00 postage & handling

Ask For: *Patterns for Pennies*

Mail To: Alpel Publishing
P.O. Box 203—PP
Chambly PQ J3L 4B3
CANADA   (postage to Canada is 40¢)

Music Brochure

Sing & Play

☆ Awaken in children a lifelong interest and ability in music. Expose them to all kinds of musical styles and incorporate music into your curriculum.

Even if you aren't particularly "musical" yourself, the **10-panel brochure** called *Share the World of Music with Your Children* can help you develop a love of music in your students. It offers specific ideas for experimenting with sound, making musical instruments, and exploring movement to music.

Send: 50¢ postage & handling

Ask For: *Share the World of Music with Your Children*

Mail To: Freebies Offer
5554 Calhoun Avenue
Van Nuys, CA 91401

Ten Tiny Erasers

A Clean Start

☆ Mistakes help kids learn, and errors can even seem fun when students have one or more of these **ten tiny erasers** in assorted shapes and sizes. Measuring just 1/2" to 3/4" each, the collectible erasers make great desk-top companions, and they're very forgiving when it comes to mistakes on schoolwork.

Send: $1.00 postage & handling

Ask For: Ten tiny erasers

Mail To: Peggy's Stuff
P.O. Box 274
Avon, MA 02322-0274

Horseshoe Rules and Information

Make a Pitch

☆ Here's a recreational activity that's as old as America itself. And the reason **horseshoe pitching** has lasted through the years is it can be fun for all ages. But while everyone is familiar with the phrase that "close only counts in horseshoes," there are other rules to the game. Before sending students out to the playground for a horseshoe tournament, send away for the rules and the other related information being offered by the National Horseshoe Pitchers Association.

Send: A long SASE

Ask For: Horseshoe Pitchers Rules, Youth Scholar-Pitcher Program and Presidential Sports Award

Mail To: National Horseshoe Pitchers Association
P.O. Box 7927
Columbus, OH 43207

Button

Good for Me!

☆ Everybody likes to be recognized for the things they do. For children, it's a valuable way of enhancing self-esteem and self-image. These **buttons with safety pin backs** do the job. One says, "World's Best Kid" in white on a red heart. The other says, "World's Smartest Kid" in blue under a graduation cap and diploma. You'll receive one of each.

Send: $2.00 for two; or $8.00 for twenty (mix or match)

Ask For: Recognition buttons

Mail To: Mr. Rainbows
Dept. S-10
P.O. Box 387
Avalon, NJ 08202

Horticulture Curriculum

Give Students Green Thumbs

☆ Teach the importance of plants and the joy of gardening with a **curriculum guide** that includes 11 perfectly planned lessons. Designed by the California Association of Nurserymen, this lesson guide uses poetry, crafts, and games to help your students develop an appreciation for horticulture. The lessons can be timed for National Gardening Month in April or can be spread out over several weeks any time of the year. The regular price is $5.00, but the supplier is offering this special discount for the readers of this book.

Send: $3.95 postage & handling

Ask For: Horticulture K-6 curriculum

Mail To: California Association of Nurserymen
4620 Northgate Blvd., Suite 155
Sacramento, CA 95834

Kid Cuisine Booklet

Keeping Up on Nutrition

☆ Clear up the confusion about proper nutrition information with a **colorful booklet** that makes sense of a healthy diet for youngsters. From new labeling laws enacted by the Food and Drug Administration to new dietary guidelines from the United States Department of Agriculture, "Kid Cuisine" is simple, direct, and easy to follow. There are no happier kids than healthy kids and a sound diet goes a long way toward keeping a smile on their young faces.

Send: Your name & address

Ask For: Kid cuisine booklet

Mail To: Kid Cuisine
"Fundamentals of Feeding Kids in the 90s"
P.O. Box 39101
Dept. 90020
Chicago, IL 60639-9946

Novelty Bracelet

Troll on a Roll

☆ Indulge a young troll lover in your life. Reward a student's classroom efforts with a **zippy troll bracelet** featuring one of the popular, furry-headed elves.

Each bracelet is a clip-on, rainbow-colored, fabric roll sporting a 1" plastic troll with unruly, brightly colored hair.

Send: $1.30 postage & handling for each bracelet

Ask For: Troll bracelet

Mail To: Marlene Monroe
6219 Ridge Manor Dr.
Memphis, TN 38115

Parent Talk

How to Talk

☆ Mistakes will be made when working with children. But with the help of *Parent Talk*, teachers and parents can keep those mistakes to a minimum.

Parent Talk is a series of articles prepared by Dr. W. Abraham of Arizona State University, a national newspaper columnist and the author of 10 books. To get an idea of the various topics available through *Parent Talk* and a **sample article,** send in for this offer.

Send: A long SASE

Ask For: *Parent Talk* sample article

Mail To: Parent Talk
Sunshine Press
P.O. Box 572
Scottsdale, AZ 85252

200 Different Stamps from Around the World

Take a World Tour

☆ Can you think of a cheap way to take your students on a trip around the world? How about a way to teach them global history and current events? The answer is philately.

Before you grab the dictionary, philately is the study of **stamps.** And you don't need a big investment to get your students started. This offer gives you 200 stamps from countries around the world including Uganda, India, Canada, and China. Studying the stamps and their designs can lead to numerous classroom discussions.

Send: $2.00 postage & handling

Ask For: 200 different stamps from around the world

Mail To: Universal
P.O. Box 466
Port Washington, NY 11050

Safety Scissors

The Cutting Edge

☆ Many parents and teachers are reluctant to let their children work with a **pair of scissors** because of safety concerns. Though a child should always learn to use scissors in the presence of an adult, these scissors are designed to minimize the risks of a new user. First, they are not sharp, second, they have rounded corners, and third, they are bendable. You will receive three pairs of these 4-1/2" long, plastic handle, colorful scissors.

Send: $1.75 for three; or $10.00 for twenty

Ask For: Safety Scissors

Mail To: Mr. Rainbows
Dept. S-8
P.O. Box 387
Avalon, NJ 08202

Ice Skates Brochure

The Cold Facts on Ice Skates

☆ Youngsters need not wait until winter to take to the ice for skating or hockey. There are numerous indoor ice rinks all across the country. For those who are serious about these two sports, they may consider purchasing their own skates. Now future skaters can pick out the perfect pair like an expert. This **informative brochure** details all the features to look for in a good pair of skates. Learn about proper size, fit, and blade types. There's also a section on ice-skating attire.

Send: A long SASE

Ask For: Buying ice skates brochure

Mail To: Ice Skating Institute of America
355 W. Dundee Road
Buffalo Grove, IL 60089-3500

Discussion Guides for Children's Books

Help Students Remember What They Read

☆ Reading is one thing. Comprehending is quite another. After your students have finished a book, there's no better way to help them understand the material than with a discussion. Three **guides** from The Reading Advantage will prepare you to lead those talks. Included are guides for "Where the Wild Things Are," "Stone Fox," and "Popper's Penguins." You'll get a summary of each book, selected questions, and topics for discussion. Each order also includes a brochure listing other discussion guides and books.

Send: $2.00 postage & handling

Ask For: Three discussion guides and brochure

Mail To: The Reading Advantage
            R.R. 3 Box 87 A, FR 5
            Hawarden, IA 51029

Store Brand Savings Guide

Go Generic

☆ The packaging may not be ornate, but the savings can be substantial. Retailers across the country offer shoppers a low-cost alternative to major-label products with their own store brands. The Private Label Manufacturers Association has a **price comparison guide** entitled *Chalk Up Back-to-School Savings With Store Brands*. It shows the big savings available on such essentials like sandwich bags, peanut butter, and multivitamins.

Send: A long SASE

Ask For: *Store Brand Savings* brochures

Mail To: Private Label Manufacturers Association
            369 Lexington Avenue
            New York, NY 10017

Educational Comics

Discovering Dinosaurs

☆ Kids read comic books, so you might as well offer them education in their favorite form.

The Tome Press is offering one **comic book** from their catalog. We looked at *Dinosaurs: An Illustrated Guide.* With a full-color cover and detailed, annotated graphics, this book will give students a good overview of the creatures which once roamed the Earth. You will also receive an illustrated catalog of other titles. Some of the titles featured are *Dante's Inferno, Jack London, Divine Comedy, King Arthur* and *Sherlock Holmes.*

Send: $1.00 for the comic book
or a long SASE for just the catalog

Ask For: Dinosaurs comic and/or Tome Press catalog

Mail To: Caliber Press
621-B S. Main Street
Plymouth, MI 48170

Paper Christmas Ornaments

Homemade Holiday Decorations

☆ When the holidays roll around, a great class project is making **Christmas decorations.** This booklet from Michelle West features some inexpensive and easy-to-make ornaments. Miniature Christmas trees, icicles, pinwheels, and birds are among the 11 fully-illustrated directions for folded-paper ornaments.

Send: $2.00 postage & handling

Ask For: *Folded Paper Christmas Ornaments* booklet

Mail To: Winslow Publishing
P.O. Box 38012-C
Toronto, ON MSN 3A8
CANADA   (postage to Canada is 40¢)

Three Recognition Certificates

Reward Students for Good Work

☆ All teachers know that a pat on the back encourages students to continue excellent work habits. Now take that pat a step further by awarding them one of these **colorful certificates for a job well done.** This packet includes three separate awards printed on heavy-duty card stock. One message offers congratulations, another recognizes good work, and the third honors neatness. Each full-color certificate is the size of a jumbo postcard (5 1/2" x 8 1/2").

Send: $2.00 postage & handling

Ask For: Three recognition certificates

Mail To: S. Brown
P. O. Box 568
Techny, IL 60082

Recyling Program

Kids Can Too

☆ Instill in students a recycling ethic and earn cash for school programs. Request this **school leader kit** for the Great Aluminum Can Roundup, a national program that turns cans into cash and helps save our landfills.

The kit contains all kinds of information to inspire you: pamphlets, tip sheets, newspaper articles, stickers, a poster, camera-ready art, charts, a press release, and a sample score sheet for tracking participation.

Send: Your name & address

Ask For: School leader kit for
the Great Aluminum Can Roundup

Mail To: CMI
1625 Massachusetts Ave., NW
Washington, DC 20036

Teaching Booklets
Making Moola

☆ When your students need some current information about **currency and coins,** be sure to have copies of these illustrated pamphlets on hand. Published by the Federal Reserve Bank of Atlanta, the thorough, eighteen-page *Fundamental Facts About U.S. Money* and the intriguing, four-page *Counterfeit?* will help you teach about the design, production, and circulation of U.S. money.

Send: Your name & address

Ask For: *Fundamental Facts About U.S. Money* and *Counterfeit?*

Mail To: Federal Reserve Bank of Atlanta
Public Affairs Department
104 Marietta Street, NW
Atlanta, GA 30303-2713

Pencil Grippers
Write Rewards

☆ Put a smile on a struggling student's face—and at the same time give him or her a helpful writing tool. Reward a pupil's efforts with one of **three pencil grippers** imprinted with a cute design and a word of encouragement.

The triangular, neon grippers allow a young student to hold a writing instrument more easily, and they add pizzazz to otherwise ordinary #2 pencils.

Send: $2.50 postage & handling for three

Ask For: Three pencil grippers with assorted imprints

Mail To: Hoyle Products, Inc.
302 Orange Grove
Fillmore, CA 93015

Book
Museum Guide

☆ This is a natural offer for educators looking to interest their students in the world around them. Titled *Natural History Museums, Volume I:* **An Illustrated Guide to Over 350 Museums in the Eastern United States,** it bears a $12.95 cover price but is available to you for just the cost of postage and handling.

Introduced by a list titled *72 Tips to Enhance Your Museum Visits*, the information appears alphabetically by state and then by city within each of the 25 eastern states.

Send: $3.00 postage & handling

Ask For: *Natural History Museum Guide Volume I*

Mail To: Batax
301 Racquet Club Rd., Suite 202
Ft. Lauderdale, FL 33326

Sea Animal Clips
Under the Sea

☆ You can almost hear the Calypso rhythms as you clip your papers with these **sea animal clips.** The little critters are made out of multi-colored foam in assorted styles including a crab, jellyfish, clam, lobster, and blowfish. They are about 1-3/4" x 2-1/4", have clips on the back, and feature little beady eyes that move.

The supplier will select one for you out of the deep blue sea.

Send: $1.95 postage & handling

Ask For: Sea animal clips

Mail To: Marlene Monroe
6210 Ridge Manor Drive/Dept. SAC
Memphis, TN 38115-3411

Recyling Lesson
Glass Class

☆ Teach your class about glass—the virtues of recycling glass, that is. Jasper Glassper, a bottle with funny glasses and a large mustache, will help you do just that. He's the central character in this **coloring book and teacher's guide** for grades K-3. You'll receive one master copy suitable for photocopying for your entire class.

Send: Your name & address

Ask For: Teacher's curriculum on recycling

Mail To: Central States Glass Recycling Program
770 E. 73rd Street
Indianapolis, IN 46240

Poetry Contest
Write & Win!

☆ The National Library of Poetry has announced that over $12,000 in prizes will be awarded to over 250 poets in the **North American Open Poetry Contest.** The contest is open to everyone and entry is free.

Any poet of any age, whether previously published or not, can be a winner. Any original poem, on any subject and in any style may be entered. The only rules are that the poem should be no more than 20 lines and the poet's name and address must appear at the top of the page. Multiple entries are permitted.

Send: Your original poem with your name and address on the page

Mail To: The National Library of Poetry
Open Poetry Contest
11419 Cronridge Drive
P.O. Box 704-Z0
Owings Mills, MD 21117

Pattern

Yesterday's News

☆ What can you take to school that won't cost you a week's salary and is easy to find? Your leftover newspapers. That's right! Take the newspapers and a stapler and have your class fold and staple their way to a wonderful **basket or box.** Send for these step-by-step, illustrated instructions that will lead them through a wonderful project they can be proud of. Plus, they're doing their part to recycle the Earth's resources. Suitable for ages eight through adult.

Send: $2.00 postage & handling

Ask For: Newspaper basket pattern

Mail To: Southwest Savvy
P.O. Box 1361-FB
Apple Valley, CA 92307

Play Cash

Funny Money

☆ When the United States mint prepares money, there are occasional overruns or errors such as smears or mistakes in cutting. That money is shredded and marked for destruction. By permission of the mint, this supplier is able to obtain this **shredded money** and offer a bag of about $10,000 of shredded bills. It can help you build a lesson plan about the mint and how money is printed.

Send: $2.00 postage & handling per bag

Ask For: Shredded money

Mail To: Bradd & Hall
1117 Jefferson Street
Lynchburg, VA 24504

Postcard Kit

Picture-Perfect Hobby

☆ Nurture your students' interest in geography and other subjects. Introduce them to deltiology, or postcard collecting, with this beginner's **postcard kit** and information on the hobby that informs collectors about history, art, architecture, geography, and famous personalities.

You'll receive five postcards from different eras and places, and you can read the information sheet supplied to figure out just when and how the cards were printed.

Send: $1.50 postage & handling

Ask For: Beginner postcard kit and information on collecting

Mail To: Joan Nykorchuk
13236 N. 7th Street, #4
Suite 237
Phoenix, AZ 85022

Keychain

Honor Troll

☆ Your entire class will try for the honor roll when they see the reward. Receive a trio of **Troll-kin key chains** to reward your students. Each of these little characters stands one and one-half inches tall and appears even taller with all the brightly colored hair sticking straight up. The key chain that comes attached to each troll figure can be removed and the troll can be used as a pencil top decoration.

Send: $2.00 postage & handling for three

Ask For: Troll-kin key chains

Mail To: E Street Gifts
716 North Ventura Road, Suite 308
Oxnard, CA 93030

Cookies

Taste of History

☆ Give your kids a taste of history. Meet the **original chocolate chip cookie,** which appeared over fifty years ago in Whitman, Massachusetts. At the Toll House Restaurant, Ruth Wakefield created the cookie quite by accident, and today it remains the world's favorite cookie.

Your students can request a 2-oz. sample bag of Original Cottage™ Cookies direct from the Toll House Bakery. Select one of two flavors: Original Chocolate Chip or Peanut Butter Chocolate Chip.

Send: $2.00 postage & handling

Ask For: 2-oz. Package of Cottage™ Cookies; Specify: Original or Peanut Butter

Mail To: Toll House Bakery Gourmet Cookie Offer
P.O. Box 457
Whitman, MA 02382

(Toll House is a service mark of Nestle Foods Corp.)

Newsletter

Power Up

☆ Science and math instructors who teach kids in grades K-6 need to understand how kids think and reason—and how to explain developments in the scientific world.

Developed with a grant from the National Science Foundation, *Power Line* is a **timely, readable newsletter** directed to elementary-level math and science teachers.

Send: Your name & address

Ask For: Sample Issue of *Power Line*

Mail To: *Power Line*
c/o Science Weekly, Inc.
2141 Industrial Parkway, Suite 202
Silver Spring, MD 20904   **Limit:** One Per Address

*Pamphlet &
Newsletter*

Frame the Fun

☆ Do you have students who need a little prodding when it comes to P.E.? Then get a little help from Bif™, who claims that bowling is a ball. Bif is the cartoon character who demonstrates **proper bowling techniques** in Bif's *Fundamentals of Bowling*, a pamphlet aimed at kids ages 3 to 21.

In addition, the alliance's eight-page newsletter called *Framework* contains helpful hints and news about other youth bowlers around the country.

Send: A Long SASE for Bif's *Fundamentals of Bowling* and a postcard for *Framework*

Ask For: *Bif's Fundamentals of Bowling* and/or *Framework*

Mail To: Young American Bowling Alliance
Attn: Bif and Buzzy
5301 South 76th Street
Greendale, WI 53129

*Sample Science
Magazine*

Factual Matters

☆ Your class can explore the extraordinary world of science with this sample issue of *Science Weekly*.

The colorful four-page **publication,** geared for specific grade levels, addresses one current science topic per issue. Each exciting edition supplies challenging exercises that test kids' science knowledge.

Send: Your name & address

Ask For: *Science Weekly*
(Please specify grade level: K through 8)

Mail To: Science Weekly, Inc.
Subscription Dept.
P. O. Box 70154
Washington, DC 20088   **Limit:** One per address

Comic book

Cent-sational!

☆ "Once Upon a Dime there was a very small island named Mazuma . . ." So opens the story depicted in the colorful, creatively conceived **comic booklet** called *Once Upon a Dime*.

Request a copy for yourself and discover an innovative way to teach young students about the basic economic concepts of barter, specialization, money, banking, central banking, and inflation.

Send: Your name & address

Ask For: *Once Upon a Dime* comic booklet

Mail To: Federal Reserve Bank of New York
Publications Section
Public Information Department
33 Liberty St.
New York, NY 10045

Puzzle

Piece of Mind

☆ Need to give your colleagues or your students a piece of your mind? Give them envelopes full of pieces. Write or draw messages on these six blank pre-cut **jigsaw puzzles.**

You can turn the white, 4" x 6" puzzles into personalized commendations for good work, special challenges for kids learning a tricky subject, anonymous notes to your principal, or novel birthday cards.

Send: $2.00 postage & handling

Ask For: Set of six jigsaw puzzles

Mail To: Jigsaw Marci
P.O. Box 914-FB
Southampton, PA 18966

Comic Book and Software

Math Laughs

☆ Innovative algebra professor Martin Weismann, nationally known for his computer tutorial software, and cartoonist Keith Monse have teamed up in their *Laugh with Math* **comic book** to make math exponentially enjoyable. The book presents such concepts as the number line and absolute values in an entertaining yet educational manner.

Along with the comic book you will receive a free algebra tutorials computer disk on a 5-1/4" floppy for the IBM and its compatibles (minimum 512K and DOS 2.11 required).

Send: $2.00 postage & handling

Ask For: *Laugh with Math* comic book and algebra tutorials computer disk

Mail To: Professor Weissman—Freebies offer
C/O Laugh & Learn
Rd #1, Box 2232
Lafayette, NJ 07848

Erasers

Tiny Tokens

☆ Even the smallest tokens of your approval build students' self-esteem. These four miniature **Christmas erasers** make perfect little rewards or gifts during the holiday season. The 3/4" erasers come in assorted, brightly colored holiday designs.

Send: 75¢ postage & handling

Ask For: Set of four mini Christmas erasers

Mail To: McVehil's Mercantile
Rd. #8, Box 112-E
Washington, PA 15301

Bookmarks

On Your Marks

☆ Inspire young readers and reward jobs well done. Get yourself a stack of these fun, two-sided **educational bookmarks** that feature cartoon-like illustrations and clever slogans.

Measuring 2-1/2" x 4-1/4", the assorted bookmarks are on neon-bright paper stock with black print.

Send: A long SASE for two bookmarks; $1.00 for ten

Ask For: Educational bookmarks

Mail To: Hungry Mind Publishing Co.
P.O. Box 14522
Philadelphia, PA 19115-0522

Cookie Cutters

Shape and Bake

☆ Contrary to what diet experts may say, it's easy to stay in shape during the holidays. With this set of six **Christmas cookie cutters,** you can bake a batch of cookies with perfect holiday shapes. In fact, you can enlist even your youngest students to roll out and bake perfectly formed edible or decorative cookies to give or to keep.

Each plastic cutter measures about three and one-half inches. The designs include a snowman, Christmas tree, teddy bear, angel, bell, and Santa.

Send: $2.00 postage & handling

Ask For: Set of six Christmas cookie cutters

Mail To: C & F Distributors
475 North Broome Ave.
Lindenhurst, NY 11757

Christmas Pencils

Write Rewards

☆ Give all your students a special Christmas treat without promoting tooth decay. Give each child a **candy-cane pencil** with a removable hook-shaped cap that allows it to hang from the classroom Christmas tree. The delightful pencils, with their red and white stripes, promote penmanship and good cheer.

Send: $1.00 postage & handling for two pencils

Ask For: Candy-cane pencils

Mail To: Eleanor Curran
530 Leonard Street, Dept. CCP
Brooklyn, NY 11222

Magazine

Something for Nothing

☆ Can your class use educational items such as: *Science Weekly*, museum guides, nutrition charts, whale activity kits, *Acorn Magazine*, cloud charts, maps, and more??

Can you use fun items such as: holiday craft projects, safety scissors, rulers, stickers, fun pencils, novelty erasers, bookmarks, and more??

Then, you need **FREEBIES magazine.** Each issue features approximately 100 useful, informative and fun items that are available for free or for a small postage and handling cost.

Send: $2.00 postage & handling for a sample issue or $5.00 for a one-year, five-issue subscription (regular rate is $8.95)

Ask For: Sample issue of *FREEBIES* or a one-year subscription as indicated above.

Mail To: *FREEBIES*/Teacher Offer
1135 Eugenia Place
Carpinteria, CA 93013

Catalog & Stickers
Unlimited Potential

☆ You'll find unlimited uses for these 240 fluorescent, three-quarter-inch **smile dot stickers.** Place them on assignments, name tags, or class charts, or award them as prizes to students who demonstrate lots of potential.

Your sticker packet will come with a full-color, 32-page catalog that offers the teaching professional additional stickers and rewards. You'll also receive a $5.00 coupon good toward your first purchase.

Send: $2.00 postage & handling

Ask For: Catalog & stickers

Mail To: Rewards Unlimited
P.O. Box 12456
Omaha, NE 68112

Dino Skeletons
Bag of Bones

☆ Create a miniature natural history museum for your classroom with this set of **six different dinosaur skeletons** made from white painted rubber. Measuring about 2-1/2" long, each miniature skeleton invites its viewers to identify the creature it represents—and to learn more about the animals that owned such bones.

Send: $1.00 postage & handling

Ask For: Six different dinosaur skeletons

Mail To: Peggy's Stuff
P.O. Box 274
Avon, MA 02322-0274

Woodpecker Toys

Pencil Friends

☆ Children reluctant to write will certainly pick up their pencils when those implements carry these clever **woodpecker pencil toys.**

Each brightly-colored toy makes his home on a plastic cap that can top a pencil's eraser. Attached to the cap is a spring on which sits a one-inch, big-eyed bird who wiggles attentively when the student writes.

Send: $1.00 postage & handling for four

Ask For: Four woodpecker pencil toys (pencils not included)

Mail To: Eleanor Curran
530 Leonard Street
Brooklyn, NY 11222

Arbor Day Planner's Kit

Plant A Tree

☆ Gather your students and your resources; send for this *Celebrate Arbor Day* packet and then get busy planting trees in your community. Prepared by the National Arbor Day Foundation, the **planner's kit** contains two posters, a newsletter, an informational pamphlet, and a 28-page booklet that offers many ideas for celebrating Arbor Day.

Just think: when you and your pupils plant trees at school or in the neighborhood, you'll combat the Greenhouse effect, provide homes for songbirds, and beautify the environment.

Send: Your name & address

Ask For: *Celebrate Arbor Day!* planner's kit

Mail To: The National Arbor Day Foundation
100 Arbor Avenue
Nebraska City, Nebraska 68410

Sample Digest
Skill Builder

☆ Build your skill at enhancing your students' communications skills. Send for a sample copy of the *ERIC®/RCS Digest* from the ERIC Clearinghouse on Reading and Communication Skills. The monthly, **two-page digest** helps educators improve the way they communicate with students so that those students will become better thinkers and communicators themselves.

Send: A long SASE

Ask For: *ERIC®/RCS Digest* info brochure

Mail To: User Services
ERIC/RCS, Stacey Silverman
Smith Research Center, Suite 150
2805 East 10th Street
Bloomington, IN 47405

Turtle Info
Turtle Troubles

☆ Send for this nifty turtle packet and receive all kinds of information about the hard-shelled creatures.

The **booklet** explains what you and your class can do to help more than 100 species of turtles that currently need protection. You will also learn where you can find even more resources covering turtles and their plight.

Send: A long SASE with two first-class stamps plus $1.00 postage & handling

Ask For: Turtle packet

Mail To: Freebies Turtle Packet
The New York Turtle & Tortoise Society
163 Amsterdam Ave., Suite 365
New York, NY 10023

Photo Holder

Tacks-Free Investment

☆ Here is the answer to one of life's vexing problems: how to display photos in the classroom or at home without damaging the walls or puncturing the pictures. It's a Tacks Free **photo mount** that allows you to post two standard-sized photographs—or the new panoramic prints—without tacks, pins, tape, or staples.

Adhere the plastic holder to your wall or refrigerator (but not to wallpaper, plasterboard, or unfinished wood), and feel free to insert or remove pictures whenever you like.

Send: $2.00 postage & handling

Ask For: Tacks Free wall-mounted photo holder

Mail To: Milt Volan
251 E. Grant Street, Dept. F
Mount Vernon, NY 10552

Booklet

Grammar School

☆ Commas, colons, semicolons, participles and gerunds leave even teachers dangling and confused. That's why this booklet is such a boon to those who want to learn **basic grammar rules.**

Grammar Basics is a pocket-sized, 15-page reference guide that covers grammar essentials. It deals with the eight parts of speech and will assist teachers and students at all grade levels.

Send: $1.75 postage & handling

Ask For: *Grammar Basics* booklet

Mail To: The Reading Advantage
1769 480th Street, Dept. FR-6
Hawarden, IL 51023

Craft Pack
Live Wires

☆ What do you do during a rainy-day recess when your students are wired but you're tired? You pull out a **craft wire kit**—or two or three—and set their imaginations free. Each package comes with one hundred feet of multicolored, plastic-coated craft wire and an idea sheet. Children can use the wire to make sculptures, baskets, and jewelry, or you can stash the wire in your drawers to take care of small repairs.

Send: $1.00 postage & handling for each kit

Ask For: Craft wire pack and idea sheet

Mail To: Alaska Craft-Wire
Box 11-1102, Dept. WR
Anchorage, AK 99511-1102

Needlepoint Kits
Festive Trio

☆ Teach yourself or your students to make delightful **needlepoint ornaments** in bright Christmas colors. Even experienced stitchers will enjoy this set of three plastic canvas needlepoint kits that arrive complete with yarn, pre-cut plastic mesh, instructions, and a needle.

Perfect as handmade gifts, the ornaments include a candy cane, wreath, and star that range in size from three to five inches.

Send: $1.50 postage & handling

Ask For: Set of three needlepoint ornament kits

Mail To: J. Preo
Dept. 25
P.O. Box 26022
Fresno, CA 93729-6022

Ice-Cream Sample

Ne-Apollo-Tan

☆ What students wouldn't love to sample honest-to-goodness astronaut food?

Request a five-eighths-ounce sample package of Neapolitan flavor **Astronaut IceCream®** and experience the delicious, freeze-dried dessert that U.S. astronauts take on their space missions. You'll discover that, as it melts in your mouth, the confection tastes amazingly like regular, earthly ice cream.

Send: $1.75 postage & handling

Ask For: Astronaut IceCream®

Mail To: Carlton Express
Dept. A
515 West Gray
Houston, TX 77019

Fingerspelling Cards

Signs of the Times

☆ It is important to be able to communicate with people who have special needs. That's why these **ABC Fingerspelling Cards** are valuable. The 100 wallet-sized cards teach the American Manual Alphabet and the hand signs for numbers one through ten so that hearing and deaf people can "talk" to each other.

The reverse side of each card describes the history of Gallaudet University, where the National Information Center on Deafness is located.

Send: $1.00 postage & handling

Ask For: ABC fingerspelling cards

Mail To: National Info. Center on Deafness
Freebies Offer/Gallaudet
800 Florida Avenue, NE
Washington, DC 20002

Seed Packets

Fast-Paced Plants

☆ Even Jack of Beanstalk fame would marvel at the growth speed from these **Hawaiian Woodrose Supervine seeds.**

Perfect for classroom gardens because they give rapid results, the Supervine grows up to four inches per day.

Each packet contains three seeds guaranteed to sprout into hardy indoor plants. Boasting deep green leaves grouped in star-like patterns, the vines prefer warm temperatures and indirect sunlight.

Send: $1.00 postage & handing

Ask For: Woodrose Supervine seeds

Mail To: Woodrose
P.O. Box 3498
San Rafael, CA 94902

No-Sew Patterns

Trash Made Tasteful

☆ Turn brown paper bags and old denim jeans or fabric remnants into "designer baskets" that look lovely and serve a purpose. Demonstrate the beauty of environmentally friendly crafts: follow these illustrated patterns for no-sew, **recycled-material earth baskets.**

Once they see what you've created, they'll want to measure, cut, and glue their own earth baskets.

Send: $1.35 postage & handling for one pattern;
$2.00 for both

Ask For: Earth basket pattern; specify jeans and/or fabric scraps pattern

Mail To: Southwest Savvy
P.O. Box 1361 F-1
Apple Valley, CA 92307

Plastic Decorations

Stik 'em Up

☆ Add some pizzazz to classroom windows or filing cabinets with the bright shapes that come on this sample sheet of STIK-EES.

Made from nonadhesive plastic, STIK-EES are **die-cut reusable stickers** that adhere with static electricity to any glossy surface. Your 5" x 6" sheet will come with STIK-EES in assorted shapes, sizes, and colors.

Send: $2.00 postage & handling

Ask For: Sample sheet of STIK-EES

Mail To: STIK-EES
788 White Street
Springfield, MA 01108

Playtime Recipes

Formula Fun

☆ *Funtime Recipes* provides creative, **nonedible recipes** that almost any child can prepare from commonly available household ingredients.

For example, you and your class can easily mix up such open-ended, creative concoctions as peanut butter playing dough and white clown make-up to while away rainy-day recesses.

This four-page leaflet has a $2.95 retail value, but any reader who mails a self-addressed stamped envelope will receive a copy for free.

Send: A long SASE

Ask For: Funtime recipes

Mail To: Funtime Recipes
P.O. Box 254
Minneapolis, MN 55423

Class Necklace
Show Some Class

☆ This item exudes class, sophistication, and charm, so it can serve as the ideal reward for excellent efforts. It's a **class-year charm necklace** that makes a great little gift for the graduate or the graduate-in-training. It looks equally smart on men and women, boys and girls.

Each charm bears numbers in shiny, thick, silver-tone metal about 1/2" long, suspended on an 18-inch chain. The charm is available for the years 1993 through 1997.

Send: $2.00 postage & handling for each set

Ask For: Class year necklace; specify '93, '94, '95, '96, or '97

Mail To: Vaughn's Gifts
739 Billy Kidd Road, Dept. N
Steens, MS 39766

Project Kit
Basket Case

☆ Here's a relaxing project to occupy your students. Their busy hands will enjoy making multicolored baskets from this woven **paper baskets kit.**

Each kit supplies enough pre-cut strips of card stock to make three baskets, each measuring about three inches square with an eight-inch handle—just the right size for carrying candy, flowers, soap, or a few Easter eggs. The instructions allow you to make more baskets from your own paper supplies.

Send: $1.00 postage & handling

Ask For: Woven paper baskets kit

Mail To: Alaska Craft Baskets Kit
Dept. PB
Box 11-1102
Anchorage, AK 99511-1102

Tip Sheets
Write Moves

☆ Move your students to write; request two **tip sheets** from award-winning author Kathy Henderson.

Ten Tips to Help Your Students Get Published offers practical suggestions for prompting students to share their written work outside contests and publications.

The second tip sheet offers guidelines for inviting professional writers into your classroom.

Send: A long SASE with two first-class postage stamps affixed

Ask For: Teachers' writing tip sheets

Mail To: Echo Communications
2151 Hale Road
Sandusky, MI 48471

Plastic Stencils
Tracing History

☆ Use this set of **six patriotic tracing figures** for classroom activities or awards. Each plastic stencil is about 3" long and comes in red, white, or blue.

You will receive one each of the following figures: George Washington, Abraham Lincoln, the nation's Capitol, the White House, the American flag and the Statue of Liberty. Or you may request stencils appropriate for a particular holiday.

Send: $1.00 postage & handling

Ask For: Six patriotic tracing figures or six holiday tracing figures (specify a single holiday)

Mail To: Peggy's Stuff
P.O. Box 274
Avon, MA 02322-0274

Eyecare Brochure

The Eyes Have It

☆ One out of every six children has a vision problem, and often that vision problem appears to be a learning disability. That's why teachers need *The ABC's of Eyecare*, a 19-page, full-color **booklet** that helps them detect vision problems, instruct youngsters about their eyes, and encourage parents to schedule annual eye checkups for their kids. The publication includes complete lesson plans for grades K to three plus a humorous 17" by 22" poster.

Send: Your name & address

Ask For: *The ABC's of Eyecare* brochure

Mail To: The ABC's of Eyecare
c/o Better Vision Institute
1800 N. Kent Street, Suite 904
Rosslyn, VA 22209   **Limit:** One per order

Award Set

Certified

☆ Certify that positive reinforcement is an important teaching tool; send for six 8-1/2" x 11" **personalized award certificates** and use them as incentives or awards.

The supplier will follow your instructions and personalize each certificate with any or all of the following information: name of recipient, name of issuer(s), date of issue, and subject of award.

Send: $1.75 postage & handling for six

Ask For: Teacher award certificates; specify personalization according to instructions above. (Please include daytime phone number for verification of unclear orders.)

Mail To: Awards Unique
P.O. Box 18822
Austin, TX 78760

Bookmark
Place-Saving Device

☆ Whenever anything interrupts your lesson, be sure to place this **magnetic bookmark** in your textbook to hold your place. Featuring a watercolor reproduction, the bookmark has a magnet on one side and a metal strip on the other. When you fold it over your page, it clasps the exact spot you choose.

Because it's magnetic, the bookmark can even lie horizontally on the page to mark the last sentence you read.

Send: $1.30 postage & handling

Ask For: Bookmark

Mail To: The Mail Bag
P.O. Box 974-BK
Claremont, CA 91711-0974

Sample Issue
Class Nuts

☆ Inspired teachers can easily inspire kids to love learning and to think imaginatively. That's why creatively conceived publications like ***Acorn Magazine*** are so valuable. Their activities encourage both teachers and kids to read and to expand their imaginations.

Full of delightful folk tales and reproducible art activities, each issue of *Acorn* centers on a particular theme that will captivate preschool and elementary-school classes.

Send: $1.50 postage & handling

Ask For: *Acorn Magazine* sample

Mail To: Bur Oak Press, Inc.
8717 Mockingbird Road South
Platteville, WI 53818

Booklet

A Matter of Facts

☆ As Sergeant Friday on the TV show *Dragnet* used to say, "The facts, ma'am. Just the facts." Here, the facts are in a new **booklet** called *The Basic Facts*, a publication supplying math, english, social studies, history, and science facts that make good quiz questions.

In the booklet you'll discover information that will interest a wide range of ages, from preschool to adult.

Send: $2.00 postage & handling

Ask For: *The Basic Facts* booklet

Mail To: The Reading Advantage
1769 480th Street, Dept. FR-6
Hawarden, IA 51023

Bookmark & Stickers

Dino-Mite Incentives

☆ Because dinosaurs and teddy bears are popular, this **mylar bookmark and sticker set** can be an effective incentive. Kids love to plaster dinosaurs and teddies on their clothing, lunch boxes, backpacks, and notebooks.

Each set includes one mylar bookmark and four matching stickers. Choose a set featuring dinosaurs in primary colors or one sporting "aerobic teddy bears" dressed for a workout.

Send: $2.00 postage & handling per set

Ask For: Mylar bookmark & stickers; specify dinosaur or teddy bear designs

Mail To: Esther's E-Z Shop
8A Village Loop Road #402
Pomona, CA 91766

Idea Booklet
Crafty Kids

☆ Turn an egg carton into a caterpillar or a potato into a pig planter. You and your youngsters can transform ordinary household materials into all kinds of imaginative projects by following the instructions in the booklet *Crafts-4-Kids*.

The **publication** describes 34 fun craft projects that require little advance preparation and are suitable for creative kids in preschool through sixth grade.

Send: $1.25 postage & handling

Ask For: *Crafts-4-Kids* booklet

Mail To: Educraft
P.O. Box 1087
Pine Valley, CA 91962

Fundraising Kit
Welcome Change

☆ Do you need money to finance a field trip or to buy teaching materials? This **sample fundraising kit** is just what you need to create a classroom cash flow—and to make your teaching more effective.

Your kit will include ideas for successful fundraisers plus three coin bags for collecting small change. Each bag displays a catchy design and a request for donations.

Send: A long SASE

Ask For: Fundraising kit—three bags and information

Mail To: The Reflectory/Moneybags
P.O. Box 1031—F92
Newburgh, NY 12550

Crochet Instructions

Hand-some Help

☆ What better way to introduce little ones to new subjects than with three-dimensional visual aids that kids can use all by themselves?

When you follow these instructions for **crocheted "occupation" hand puppets** you'll have exactly that: user-friendly, 11-inch puppets that students can use to create all kinds of scenarios.

Crochet a doctor/dentist, nurse, fire fighter, police officer, father, mother, boy, or girl.

Send: A long SASE

Ask For: Crochet instructions for "occupation" hand puppets

Mail To: Lorraine Vetter
7924-H Soper Hill Road
Everett, WA 98205

Info Card

Make Waves

☆ Introducing shortwave radio into your school or curriculum is fairly easy and inexpensive, and this *Shortwave Frequency Bands and Users* **info card** lists what kinds of broadcasts—including those from foreign countries—are out there.

You'll also receive a pamphlet that describes the informative book *Shortwave Goes to School—A Teacher's Guide to Using Shortwave Radio in the Classroom.*

Send: $1.00 postage & handling per card

Ask For: Shortwave info card and *Shortwave Goes to School* pamphlet

Mail To: Tiare Publications
P.O. Box 493
Lake Geneva, WI 53147

Color & Learn Book

Down On Drugs

☆ The copyrighted *Say No to Drugs* **color and learn book** for grades K-6 invites frank discussions between adults and kids about the differences between "good" and "bad" drugs, and between prescription medications and illegal substances. Featuring clowns who impart lessons, the 16-page booklet includes puzzles, games, and facts that encourage "prevention now instead of correction later."

Send: $2.00 postage & handling for one book

Ask For: The *Say No to Drugs* color and learn book

Mail To: Milt Volan
251 E. Grand Street, Dept. F
Mount Vernon, NY 10552

Sticker Kit

Smiling Faces

☆ Start the year on a cheery note: send for a **smiling faces welcome kit** and bring some smiles to your new students' faces.

Each kit includes two 5" x 3-1/2" place cards brightly decorated with colorful smiley faces plus a sheet of 20 little smiling stickers you can stick on name tags, shirts, or papers.

Send: $1.50 postage & handling

Ask For: Smiling faces welcome kit

Mail To: Smiles Unlimited
Smiling Faces Welcome Kit
2849 Dundee Road, Suite 140F
Northbrook, IL 60062

Award Diplomas

Proud Papers

☆ These assorted **recognition award diplomas** are excellent ways to express your admiration for scholastic excellence. Bright, colorful, and funny, the diplomas come in five versions, from which you choose two.

Boost your students' confidence by selecting "Reading Award," "Spelling Wizard," "Neatness Award," "Congratulations, you did it!", or "Good Work, keep it up!"

Send: $1.00 postage & handling for two

Ask For: Recognition award diplomas; specify any two versions

Mail To: First Express
Certificate Offer
2849 Dundee Road, Suite 140
Northbrook, IL 60062

Calculator Eraser

Mistakes Happen

☆ Everyone is prone to the occasional mistake and students are no exception. A handy item for clearing up errors is an eraser. Teachers can get a pack of **three rubber erasers,** all shaped and imprinted to look like calculators. They would make great awards for those winning class competitions or they could serve as a delicate reminder to those who need to be extra careful.

Send: $1.20 postage & handling

Ask For: Set of Three Calculator Erasers

Mail To: Marlene Monroe
Dept. Calculator Erasers
6210 Ridge Manor Drive
Memphis, TN 38115-3411

Portable Office Guide

Home Work Help

☆ Students spend as much time at home working on assignments as they do in the classroom. Teachers also find themselves bringing work home. Sharp Electronics has designed a **step-by-step guide to selecting office equipment** in the aptly titled *The Age of the Portable Office*. This eight-page booklet highlights important issues to consider when purchasing the components needed for working at home or school.

Send: A long SASE

Ask For: *The Age of the Portable Office* guide

Mail To: Sharp Electronic Corp.
P.O. Box 3900
Peoria, IL 61614

Musical Note Erasers

Wipe Out

☆ If you want to strike the right note with students, order a set of **erasers shaped like musical notes.** You can use these colorful erasers in many different ways. Use them to stimulate a student's interest in music. Give one to a student who consistently gets good grades on quizzes or homework. In fact, you may even need to keep one or two for yourself. Just in case.

Send: $1.00 postage & handling

Ask For: Four Musical Note Erasers

Mail To: Marlene Monroe
Dept. Musical Note Erasers
6210 Ridge Manor Drive
Memphis, TN 38115-3411

Young Folks Genealogy Package

Study the Family Tree

☆ More and more students are showing interest in their family heritage. Here's a great way to nurture this natural curiosity and offer a history lesson in the bargain. The **Young Folks Genealogy Package** was designed to help students research their family history. The program was successfully tested at the fifth grade level and comes complete with instructions, an outline of family research, and an ancestor chart. This would make either a great classroom activity or a term project.

Send: $2.00 postage & handling

Ask For: Young Folks Genealogy Package

Mail To: Leonard Data Quest
P.O. Box 212-FFM
Staunton, IL 62088

100 Different Foreign Nature Stamps

Miniature Nature Scenes

☆ There are several excellent ways to illustrate various aspects of nature for your students. You could buy expensive textbooks, or order this collection of **foreign postage stamps** with various nature designs.

The colorful graphics on these stamps from countries around the world include drawings of birds, butterflies, plants, and mountain vistas. Beyond nature, these stamps offer a few lessons on history and geography as well.

Send: $2.00 postage & handling

Ask For: 100 foreign country nature stamps

Mail To: Nature Stamps
P.O. Box 466
Port Washington, NY 11050

Memo Books
Take Note

☆ Do your students have trouble remembering to complete assignments? Reward those who *do* remember by giving them one of three **mini dinosaur memo books.**

Each cheerful, 2-1/2" x 3-1/2" pad contains 20 pages of ruled paper. The spiral-bound notebooks, which feature cartoon-like dinosaurs on their covers, will certainly reinforce your students' need to write down their assignments.

Send: $1.00 postage & handling for three

Ask For: Mini dinosaur memo books

Mail To: Eleanor Curran
530 Leonard Street
Brooklyn, NY 11222

Dog Erasers
Dog Gone-It

☆ One day before break and your student is working on a term paper due tomorrow. Dissatisfied with the results, the student reaches for one of these **dog shaped erasers,** deletes any mistakes, and continues the assignment with renewed spirit.

The supplier will select two erasers from a colorful canine collection that includes a shaggy sheepdog, a pug-face boxer, and others. Fetch yourself a set of these puppies today.

Send: $1.50 postage & handling

Ask For: Dog Erasers

Mail To: Marlene Monroe
Dept. Dog Erasers
6210 Ridge Manor Drive
Memphis, TN 38115-3411

*Consumer Budget
Planner*

Budget
A Bit

☆ Everyone seems to be having trouble making ends meet. Students who can't seem to hold onto their money should consider budgeting. Sounds complicated, but not when you order this helpful **Consumer Budget Planner** from the Consumer Credit Foundation.

This basic guide for budgeting includes information on setting financial goals, keeping track of expenditures, and charting special expenses. The brochures include easy instructions, tips, and charts.

Send: A long SASE

Ask For: Consumer Budget Planner
(Also available in Spanish on request)

Mail To: Consumer Credit Education Foundation
Dept. CBP
919 18th Street NW
Washington, DC 20006

Stickers

Global
Awareness

☆ This set of **12 EarthSeals stickers** will remind you and your students to take care of our environment.

An appropriate reward for a noteworthy science paper or project, each 2" circular sticker shows a colorful NASA photograph of our planet.

Send: A long SASE plus $2.00 donation would be appreciated by this organization

Ask For: EarthSeals stickers

Mail To: EarthSeals
P.O. Box 8000-FRB
Berkeley, CA 94707

Potpourri Sachet Kit

It Makes Scents

☆ Here's an idea for a class project just in time for Valentine's Day. Have students make their own **potpourri sachets** from this kit. The sachets are styled like a Victorian ball or shaped like a heart. Students can hang them in closets and bedrooms to add a special scent to the air or give them as a gift.

The sachet kits come complete with fragrant potpourri, lace, tulle, ribbon, beads, and instructions. All you need to add is a little time, scissors, and a drop of glue.

Send: $2.00 postage & handling

Ask For: Potpourri Sachet Kit
(Specify victorian ball or heart-shaped)

Mail To: Southwest Savvy
P.O. Box 1361, F-4
Apple Valley, CA 92307

Food Stickers

Sticky Reminders

☆ October may be Nutrition Month, but you can use these stickers as reminders or rewards any time of year. You'll receive two packs of **sticker sheets,** each containing a dozen stickers shaped like hamburgers, hot dogs, ice-cream cones, and other tasty treats. Use them to show your satisfaction for a homework assignment well done.

Send: $1.00 postage & handling

Ask For: Two Packets of Food Stickers

Mail To: Marlene Monroe
Dept. Food Stickers
6210 Ridge Manor Drive
Memphis, TN 38115-3411

Seed Packet
Up a Tree

☆ Teach some botany or basic biology by growing a fruit tree in the classroom. Not enough room, you say? Then try growing a tomato tree from this packet of **tomato tree seeds.**

The tomato tree is native to South America that grows up to ten feet tall indoors or out, and it produces large, exotic leaves followed by fragrant flowers which become beautiful red fruit that one can eat raw or cooked.

Send: $1.00 postage & handling

Ask For: Tomato tree seeds

Mail To: Tomato Tree
               P.O. Box 3498
               San Rafael, CA 94902

Stuffed Heart Wreath Kit

Hearts On The Mend

☆ How can you mend a broken heart? Simple, get a needle and stitch together in a circle the individual, stuffed fabric hearts that make up this **mini heart wreath kit.**

Just in time for Valentine's Day, you and your students can make a lovely wreath consisting of six 3"-wide pre-sewn hearts, which joined together form a wreath measuring 8" in diameter. The kit comes with everything you need to complete this simple project in a few heartbeats.

Send: $1.75 postage & handling

Ask For: Stuffed Heart Wreath Kit

Mail To: The Crafter's Cottage
               345 S. McDowall Blvd., Suite 314
               Petaluma, CA 94954

Bendable Graduation Figure

Grads Rule

☆ Here's one way to let your graduates know that they have achieved some measure of success. Give them a big, **bendable graduation figure** as a gift.

This 6" tall character looks like a ruler with arms, legs, face and a diploma in one hand. The rubber figure is molded on a flexible wire frame that allows it to be bent into all sorts of poses.

Send: $1.75 postage & handling

Ask For: Bendable Graduation Figure

Mail To: The Complete Collegiate
490 Route 46 East
Fairfield, NJ 07004

Dorm Essential Catalog

The Good Life

☆ Living away from home during that first year of college can be a rewarding experience, especially with a little planning. Stock up on everything you need by going through this 12-panel *Complete Collegiate Dorm Essentials* **catalog.** It comes with a handy checklist that tells students what they should bring to their new dorm room and allows them to order anything they don't already have. One featured item is a two-sided laundry bag so they can separate their light and dark clothing. If they're smart enough to get into college, ordering this brochure will be a wise investment of time.

Send: A long SASE

Ask For: *Dorm Essential Catalog* w/checklist

Mail To: The Complete Collegiate
P.O. Box 1543
West Caldwell, NJ 07007-1543

Poetry Contest
Prizes for Poets

☆ Do you have a prize-winning poem? You won't know unless you enter the **Sparrowgrass Poetry Forum contest.** All poets are encouraged to submit a poem. There is no cost to enter the contest. A prize of $500 is given to the first-place winner and additional cash prizes are also awarded.

To enter this on-going contest, send in one original poem (amateur or professional) of 20 lines or less and your name and address.

Send: Your original poem with your name and address.

Mail To: Sparrowgrass Poetry Forum
Dept. FS
203 Diamond Street
Sistersville, WV 26175

Scratch 'n Sniff Stickers
Teaching "In-scent-ives"

☆ You might think fish smell unpleasant. But that's not the case with these adorable, multicolored **scratch 'n sniff sea creature stickers.** These unique button-sized stickers have six different cute designs on them and smell like berries when you scratch them.

Give them to your students as incentives. They're great for decorating binders, papers or just to brighten up somebody's day. And they may encourage students to keep their noses in their books.

Send: $1.00 for 88 stickers; $2.00 for 264

Ask For: Scratch 'n Sniff stickers

Mail To: The Very Best, Dept. FF
P.O. Box 2838
Long Beach, CA 90801-2838

Herb Seeds
Watch Your Garden Grow

☆ You can grow your very own basil, parsley, thyme, chives, and sage right in your classroom as a science or gardening project. You will receive **herb seeds** for the five herbs listed and the rest is up to you. Pick a windowsill and have fun watching the plants sprout and grow.

Send: $2.00 postage & handling

Ask For: 5 herb seeds

Mail To: Childs Company
Dept. Herbs
P. O. Box 3498
San Rafael, CA 94912

Postcard Set
Civil War Events

☆ Here's a **unique postcard set** that could be put to good use with a class that is studying the Civil War period. Each of the seven Civil War postcards depicts a different major event as portrayed in authentic newspapers of the time.

The postcards are black and white and have illustrations as well as copy taken from actual newspapers. The reverse side of each card denotes some specific details of the event portrayed on the picture side of the card.

Send: $1.60 postage & handling

Ask For: Civil War postcards

Mail To: Esther's E-Z Shop
Dept. Postcards
P. O. Box 1831
Pomona, CA 91769

Science Experiment
Like Magic

☆ This **super science experiment** is sure to perk up even your most disinterested students. You will receive a sample of crystals along with instructions for several different experiments, all involving ordinary household items. Watch the crystals expand, grow, and change colors. They are nontoxic and environmentally safe. This kit is offered by the author of five award-winning science books for ages 4–14 who is making this special science experiment just for the readers of this book.

Send: $2.00 postage & handling

Ask For: Crystal experiment

Mail To: The Backyard Scientist
Dept. Freebies crystals
P. O. Box 16966
Irvine, CA 92713

Ruler & Pencil
Measure of Patriotism

☆ To pay tribute to our country's leaders, hold a civics contest and give out prizes like this **patriotic ruler and pencil set.**

The plastic 12-inch ruler bears on one side the pictures, names, and terms of office of our nation's Presidents. The flip side displays six of our country's flags plus historical notes and the words to "The Star-Spangled Banner."

With the ruler comes a stars-and-stripes pencil.

Send: $2.55 postage & handling

Ask For: Patriotic pencil and 12-inch ruler

Mail To: The Mail Bag
P.O. Box 974-PR
Claremont, CA 91711-0974

Award Stickers
Great Jobs

☆ When your students have done an outstanding job, what do you reward them with? Most of the neat little prizes you find are too expensive. Here's just the right reward for the right price. You can have a set of ten round **stickers** that are 1-1/2" around, are very colorful, and have sayings such as: "#1," "Great Job," "A+," and more. You may order as many sets as you like so there's enough for your whole classroom.

Send: $1.00 postage & handling for each set of ten

Ask For: School design round stickers

Mail To: Lightning Inc.
P. O. Box 16121
West Palm Beach, FL 33416

Postcard Set
Great Moments

☆ Space exploration has provided us with many thrilling moments. If your students are learning about the great moments in space then send for this set of **space history postcards.** You'll receive six different cards; each depicting a front page of a major U. S. newspaper with a special moment in space history prominently featured. Most of the cards feature color photographs of the events they cover.

Send: $1.60 postage & handling

Ask For: Space history postcards

Mail To: Esther's E-Z Shop
Dept. Space cards
P. O. Box 1831
Pomona, CA 91769

Praise Stickers

U-R Great

☆ **Star-shaped stickers** have always been thought of as the best reward. Whether it's for good attendance or a great improvement in writing skills, the star sticker will let your students know they've been doing a good job. You can have a set of ten assorted star stickers that are 1-1/2" in size and they contain sayings such as: "Outstanding Work," "U-R Great" and "Write On." You may order as many sets as you like.

Send: $1.00 postage & handling for each set of ten

Ask For: Star-shaped praise stickers

Mail To: Lightning Inc.
P. O. Box 16121
West Palm Beach, FL 33416

Pencils

Write Motivation

☆ Give your students the "write idea"—let them know you're proud of their efforts—with these bright and bold **incentive pencils.** Whether it be English or Math or any other subject, your kids will be inspired to do their best when offered these terrific rewards.

Made in the U.S.A., these No. 2 pencils come in a variety of eye-catching colors—even the erasers are colored in most cases. All come decorated with assorted imprinted designs and sayings such as "Student of the Week" and "Excellent Work."

Send: $1.00 postage & handling for three; $2.50 for a dozen

Ask For: Incentive pencils

Mail To: Peggy's Stuff
P.O. Box 274
Avon, MA 02322-0274

FREE   FREE   FREE

Something for nothing!! Hundreds of dollars worth of items in each issue of **FREEBIES MAGAZINE.** Five times a year, for over 14 years, each issue features at least 100 FREE and low-postage-&-handling-only offers. Useful, informative, and fun items. Household information, catalogs, recipes, health/medical information, toys for the grandchildren, samples of every–thing from tea bags to jewelry—every offer of every issue is yours for FREE, or for a small postage and handling charge (never more than $2.00)!

Have you purchased a "Free Things" book before—only to find that the items were unavailable? That won't happen with FREEBIES—all of our offers are authenticated (and verified for accuracy) with the suppliers!

- -

SPECIAL OFFER FOR TEACHERS

☑ YES - Send me 5 issues for only $5.00 (save 60% off the cover price and save $3.95 off the regular subscription rate!)

☐ Payment Enclosed, or charge my   ☐ VISA ☐ MasterCard

Card Number _ _ _ _ _ _ _ _ _ _ _ _ _ _ _ _   Exp. Date _ _ _ _

Name_____ | Daytime phone #

Address_____ | ( )_____

City_____ State _____ Zip_____ | (in case we have a question about your subscription)

Send to: FREEBIES MAGAZINE/Teacher Offer
1135 Eugenia Place, Carpinteria, CA 93013